Hawaii's Volcanoes

by Marjorie Frank

Houghton Mifflin Harcourt™

PHOTOGRAPHY CREDITS: COVER ©Michael T. Sedam/Corbis; 3 (bl) ©Allan Baxter/ImageBank/Getty Images; 10 (b) ©Digital Vision/Getty Images; 11 (t) ©Jerry Alexander/Getty Images; 13 (t) ©Michael T. Sedam/Corbis

Printed in the U.S.A.

ISBN: 978-0-544-07295-4

12 13 14 15 16 17 18 19 20   1083   20 19 18

4500710511   B C D E F G

Contents

Vocabulary

volcano

mountain

earthquake

canyon

Stretch Vocabulary

dormant   current

inner core   crust

outer core   tectonic plates

mantle

Introduction

There are many volcanoes in the United States. A few of them are still active and will erupt. But most have been dormant for thousands of years or more. Dormant means not active.

Hawaii is different. Hawaii is the only U.S. state made up entirely of volcanoes! Some are still active. In fact, two have erupted in the last 50 years. (Alaska and Washington are the only other states where volcanoes have erupted recently.)

Here's what this means: If you visit Hawaii, you will be standing on a volcano. If you live in Hawaii, you *live* on a volcano!

Don't let the green hills and the lush forests fool you. Each and every Hawaiian island is a mountain rising from the ocean floor, and each of them was formed from a volcano.

The peaceful island of Oahu was once a fiery volcano.

You Are Floating on a Plate

To understand the story of Hawaii's volcanoes, you need to know something about what's below your feet—way below.

If you could cut Earth in half, it would look a little like an onion. At the center is a ball of solid iron that is about as hot as the surface of the sun. This is Earth's inner core. The outer core—a layer of liquid iron—surrounds the inner core.

The next layer is called the mantle. The mantle is made of very hot solid rock. This rock is so hot that it flows the way thick, hot taffy candy might flow. In some places, the slow movement creates a kind of current—a flow of matter in a particular direction.

Next is Earth's crust. The crust includes Earth's surface. It is made up of the soil and rocks you know so well. The seafloor, or bottom of the ocean, is part of Earth's surface.

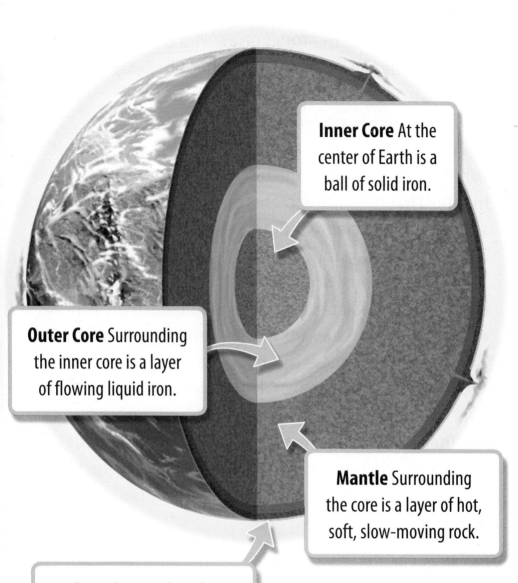

Inner Core At the center of Earth is a ball of solid iron.

Outer Core Surrounding the inner core is a layer of flowing liquid iron.

Mantle Surrounding the core is a layer of hot, soft, slow-moving rock.

Crust Surrounding the mantle is a layer of solid rock reaching to the surface.

Earth Is Moving under Your Feet

The crust is not one solid piece. The crust and part of the mantle below is broken into huge pieces called tectonic plates. Texas is on the North American plate. The Hawaiian Islands are on the Pacific plate.

Tectonic plates are like pieces of a jigsaw puzzle. Together, they float on the taffy-like material of the mantle. That means the plates actually move, but they do so very slowly. Scientists figure that plates move about 2–3 inches a year, about as fast as your fingernails grow.

However, plates don't all move in the same direction. In some places, plates are crashing into each other. In other places, plates are splitting apart or grinding past each other. Where this happens, rocks can break suddenly. The earth shakes. Huge cracks in the land can appear. Earthquake!

Where plates crash together or split apart, rock deep underground can melt. It may rise up through cracks and burst through to the surface. Hot lava may pour out from inside Earth. Volcano!

Most earthquakes and volcanoes happen in places where plates meet. Many happen along the border of the Pacific plate. This area is called the Ring of Fire. The red marks on the map show where volcanoes have erupted. See how they follow the border of the Pacific plate?

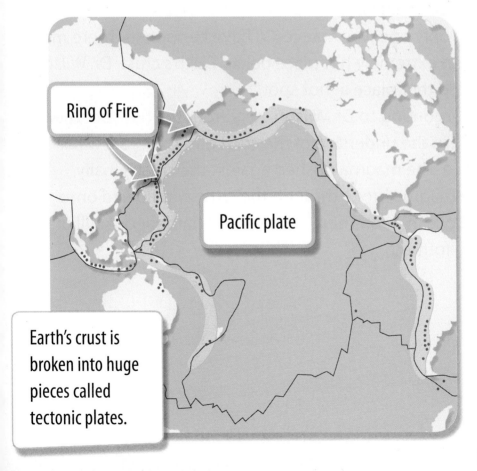

Ring of Fire

Pacific plate

Earth's crust is broken into huge pieces called tectonic plates.

Blame It on the Hot Spot!

The Hawaiian Islands are on the Pacific plate, but they are not near the Ring of Fire. Yet the Hawaiian Islands were formed by volcanoes. In fact, they are still being formed today. What caused the volcanoes that created these islands? Canadian scientist J. Tuzo Wilson came up with an idea that helped answer this question. His idea became known as the "hot spot" theory.

Dr. Wilson observed that some of Hawaii's volcanoes had been active for a very long time. He thought there was only one way that could have happened. There must be an extremely hot place below Earth's crust. Dr. Wilson called that place a "hot spot."

According to Dr. Wilson, heat from the hot spot melted rock in the underside of the crust and created a weak place. The magma pushed against the crust. Finally, the magma broke through the crust and flowed onto the ocean floor. Then it cooled and hardened. A hill of lava formed.

The Hawaiian Islands follow the path of the Pacific plate over a hot spot.

Dr. Wilson reasoned that, at first, the hill was very small. Over time more eruptions took place. With each eruption, the bump grew bigger. After a very long time, it was no longer just a bump on the floor of the ocean. It was big enough to break the surface of the water. It was an island.

If you look at a map, you'll see that Hawaii has eight islands, not one. Does that mean there are eight hot spots, one for each island? Dr. Wilson didn't think so.

Dr. Wilson knew that Earth's tectonic plates float on the mantle. His idea was that the hot spot stayed in one place. The Pacific plate moved.

As the Pacific plate moved, the island that was on it also moved. After a very long time, the island moved away from the hot spot and stopped growing. As a new part of the plate reached the hot spot, a new island began to form.

Westward Bound

The Pacific plate moves to the west and to the north. If Dr. Wilson's theory is right, the island farthest west should be the oldest.

Kauai meets that description perfectly. It is the farthest west of all the islands. It is also the oldest. If you have watched the film *Jurassic Park*, you have seen parts of Kauai.

Kauai is about five million years old. But it has been dormant for a long time. The last eruption on Kauai took place about 400,000 years ago.

Many scientists believe that Kauai started out where Hawaii Island is now. Over time, Kauai moved to its present location—about 300 miles west and north.

Over time, erosion has carved creases into Kauai's rock formations. Kauai is eroded more than the younger islands.

The depth of Waimea Canyon is another way Kauai shows its age.

Kauai has more erosion than the other islands. That shouldn't be surprising. Since it's the oldest, wind and water have had more time to wear away bits of land.

In addition, Kauai has a very wet climate. In fact, Mount Waialeale—an old volcanic mountain on the island—is one of the wettest places on Earth. Mount Waialeale is in the middle of Kauai. From there, many streams flow downhill. The streams carry bits and pieces of the mountain with them.

Over time, erosion has carved the steep sides of Waimea Canyon. Waimea Canyon is almost half a mile deep. It is known as the Grand Canyon of the Pacific. You can see red lava rock from ancient eruptions all along the sides of the canyon.

The Mountain with Wet Feet

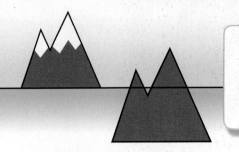

Measured from the seafloor, Mauna Loa is the tallest mountain on Earth. It is taller than Mt. Everest.

According to Dr. Wilson's theory, the island farthest east should be the youngest island. And it is! That island is Hawaii, or the "Big Island," as it is sometimes called.

Hawaii began forming about 700,000 years ago. It is made up of five different volcanoes. Two of them are still active—Mauna Loa and Kilauea. Mauna Loa erupted three times during the 1900s. The last eruption was in 1984.

Mauna Loa is a shield volcano. That means its slopes are not steep. If you look at it from the side, you will see that it is actually shaped like a shield.

The name Mauna Loa means "Long Mountain." Mauna Loa is one of the biggest mountains on Earth. Its peak rises about ten and a half miles above the ocean floor. If Mount Everest—the highest mountain above sea level— were placed next to Mauna Loa, Mauna Loa would tower over it.

Kilauea is the youngest Hawaiian volcano and one of the most active in the world.

Kilauea is the youngest volcano on Hawaii, and it is the farthest east. It may also be the most active volcano in the world. Since 1952, Kilauea has erupted 34 times. The last eruption started in 1983 and is still going on!

Most Kilauea eruptions are gentle—no bang, no big burst, very little noise. A Kilauea eruption is mostly steam and a stream of fiery lava that shoots several feet into the air. The lava flows downhill. It cools and hardens. Each time it erupts, Kilauea grows some more.

An Island in the Making

Another Hawaiian island is forming right now. Its name is Loihi. At the moment, Loihi is only a seamount. A seamount is an underwater mountain.

Loihi rises less than a mile from the ocean floor. Even so, it is taller than many peaks that have their bases on dry land. And Loihi is still growing. If it keeps on growing, it may become the next Hawaiian island.

Loihi is at the southern end of a long chain of volcanoes—eighty in all. Some, like Hawaii, are islands. Others, like Loihi, are seamounts. The volcanoes form a trail from Hawaii all the way to Alaska.

The volcanoes in the chain began forming seventy million years ago. Their positions show how the Pacific plate has moved.

If the plate keeps moving, Hawaii may be carried past the hot spot. Its volcanoes may become dormant. A new island may form over the hot spot. But it won't happen anytime soon.

Make a Model

You can make your own volcano erupt! Mix together 3 cups of flour with 1 cup of salt and 1 cup of water. Next, fill a small bottle ¾ full of hot water from the tap. Add a squirt of liquid soap and 2 tablespoons of baking soda. Set the bottle in a large dish or pan. Next, press your dough around the bottle, making sure not to plug the opening. Pour a little vinegar in the opening of the bottle. Watch your volcano erupt!

Write an Explanation

Imagine yourself as a writer who works for a tour company in Hawaii. Write a brochure explaining what you know about volcanoes. Explain to visitors why it is that they do not need to be afraid of Hawaii's volcanoes. Include any rules and precautions that might help keep tourists safe.

Glossary

canyon [KAN•yuhn] A valley with steep sides.

crust [CRUST] The solid, outermost part of Earth.

current [KUR•ent] A part of water or air that moves in a certain direction.

dormant [DOHR•mehnt] Not active.

earthquake [ERTH•kwayk] A shaking of Earth's surface that can cause land to rise and fall.

inner core [IN•ur KAWR] The solid, deepest part of Earth's core, consisting mostly of the metal iron.

mantle [MAN•tuhl] The layer of Earth's interior between the outer core and the crust.

mountain [MOUNT•uhn] The highest kind of land, with sides that slope toward its top.

outer core [OW•tur KAWR] The liquid-iron layer of Earth between the mantle and the inner core.

tectonic plates [tek•TAHN•ik PLAYTS] The large, plate-like pieces of Earth's crust and mantle that move slowly.

volcano [vahl•KAY•noh] A mountain made of lava, ash, or other materials from eruptions.